THE ROAD TO BODNANT

Henry Davis Pochin
Founder of Bodnant Garden
(*From a bust in Salford Town Hall*)

THE

ROAD TO BODNANT

THE STORY BEHIND THE
FOUNDATION OF THE FAMOUS
NORTH WALES GARDEN

H. T. Milliken

1975
E. J. MORTEN

Published by
E. J. Morten
10 Warburton Street, Didsbury
Manchester 20

H. T. Milliken 1975

ISBN 0 85972 021 7

Printed in Great Britain by
The Scolar Press Limited, Ilkley, Yorkshire

TO MY WIFE

ACKNOWLEDGEMENTS

During the writing of this story I have received much help from many sources including the Libraries of Leicester, Manchester, Salford, Prestatyn, Conway, Eccles, Wandsworth and Richmond-upon-Thames. The House of Commons Library, through the courtesy of Mr. Lewis Carter-Jones, M.P., also supplied valuable information as did the Public Records Office, The Companies Record Office, Chetham's Library, Pochin & Co., English China Clays, Lovering & Pochin and the Staveley Iron & Coal Company. Above all my thanks are due to Miss M. Patry, B.A., F.L.A., Assistant Manager (Libraries), Salford Metropolitan Cultural Services, for her invaluable guidance during the preparation of the original manuscript.

INTRODUCTION

Born in the tiny village of Wigston, near Leicester, on the 25th May, 1824, Henry Davis Pochin, the son of a farmer whose family had lived in the district for 200 years, achieved during his lifetime a success that, judged even by modern standards, is remarkable. With no education other than that received in the local schools, or by private study, he became the founder of a very profitable chemical business with branches in several towns and china-clay mines in Cornwall, a leading industrialist, and a promoter of companies whose total registered capital exceeded £7,000,000.

At one time he was a director of no less than twenty-two companies and a Chairman or Vice-Chairman of several of them, including John Brown & Co., the Steelmakers of Sheffield, Bolckow Vaughan & Co., the Ironmasters of Middlesbrough, the Staveley Iron & Coal Company, Palmers Shipbuilding and Iron Company, and the Metropolitan Railway Company.

He became a Member of Parliament, a Mayor of the city in which he had his chemical works, a Justice of the Peace and a Sheriff of the County to which he retired.

His business exploits and his other activities may by now have been largely forgotten but his name is still remembered by many of the thousands of people who, each year, visit the famous gardens at Bodnant, near Conway, North Wales, that he laid out in 1875. As the Centenary of the gardens approaches it is appropriate that the story of his success should be recalled and a tribute paid to a man who, by his imagination, application, and inventiveness, achieved such remarkable results.

CHAPTER I

Little is known of Henry Davis Pochin's early life beyond the fact that at the age of thirteen he was sent by his father, William Pochin, to the Proprietary School at Leicester for his "finishing off" education. The school had about 73 pupils and catered, according to its prospectus, "for the needs of those who desire for their children a sound classical education with those studies which especially qualify for the pursuits of an active and commercial life." Natural History and Science loomed largely in the school's curriculum. Himself a radical, William Pochin had a financial interest in the school, which had been established with some difficulty after an abortive attempt had been made by the Radicals and Conservatives in the district to form a joint school to replace the existing but declining Grammar school.

The younger Pochin, who for a time resided at the house of the Second Master whilst he was at the Proprietary School, remained there for less than a year and was then, in the mid-summer of

THE SALE WILL TAKE PLACE

IN THE TOWN HALL,

To commence at TWO o'clock in the Afternoon.—Conditions as usual, and no Reserve.

1st.—Five block tin Tea Kettles, 1 iron ditto, and 4 Water Cans.

The cans are well painted, and all of the above are of the best materials. From Mr. BAINES'S, Brazier, High-street. Rate, 7s. 7¼d.

2nd.—Six superior Gentlemen's Hats, 6 dozen black Stockings, 1 dozen white cotton ditto, and 11 pair of Men's drab ditto.

Any Gent. requiring a church-going Hat will do well to attend this sale, they being of very modern shape; the stockings are of the best quality, and are recommended to any Lady requiring the same. These are from Messrs. W. and G. BAINES'S, Market Place, in the Borough of Leicester. Rate, 28s. 9d.

3rd.—Two scrub Brushes, and 2 sweeping ditto, made of the strongest and best of bristles; also, 2 prime new milk Cheese.

These are from Mr. THIRLBY'S, Grocer, High-street, Leicester. Rate, 5s. 7¼d.

4th.—Four reams of strong and very tuff Paper.

From a Gentleman whose name is J. F. WINKS, High-street, Leicester. The demand from this Gentleman for the Church-rate, 6s.

5th.—Ten pair of well-shaped Ladies' Shoes, and 6 pair strong Women's leather ditto.

These are imported (duty free,) into the Lock-up, Town Hall Lane, from Mr. JOHN HOLMES, Silver-street, Leicester. The Ladies are most respectfully invited to these lots, and are assured that they shall go duty free. Rate, 11s. 3d.

6th.—Handsome Spanish Mahogany Pembroke Table, with Drawer, on brass castors.

This lot is fit to grace the study of any Clergyman, having arrived from Mr. JOHN PICKARD'S, Market-place, Leicester. Rate, 1s. 6d.

7th.—A very sweet lot—viz. 2 large loaves of fine Lump Sugar.

Imported by Mr. JOHN MANNING, Tea Dealer, High-street, Leicester. This is a rare opportunity for Teetotalers! Rate, 12s.

8th.—Ten Ladies' Dresses; also, 150 yards of really good Calico.

The Ladies will find this an opportunity which perhaps may never occur again. The Auctioneer particularly requests an inspection of these dresses, as they are of a superior quality and design, and have been imported so lately as Monday the 7th inst. from Messrs. T. & W. STEVENSON'S, Market Place, Leicester. Rate, 21s. 1¼d.

9th.—One 9-pint and three 8-pint copper Tea Kettles, two Watering Pans, and Chamber Bucket.

The copper tea kettles are very superior; have arrived from Mr. JAMES SHARDLOW'S, East-gates, Leicester. Rate, 14s. 7¼d.

10th.—Five prime old Cheese, now in the Lock-up, and will be tried on Monday next.

Late the property of Messrs. SWAIN and PADBY, Cheese Factors and Tea Dealers, Highcross-street. Mr. Swain's private Rate, 7s. 6d.; the Firm's Rate, 13s. 3d.

11th.—(And last, it may be hoped,) Half-dozen strong Windsor Chairs, deal Kitchen Table, and a very handsome Norway oak Stand.

These have been taken from Mr. H. A. COLLIER, Mercury Office, High-street, Leicester. Rate, 8s. 6d.

A common form of protest amongst the radicals of Leicester was a refusal to pay Church Rates, a form of local taxation levied for the purpose of raising funds for the Established Church. The penalty for non-payment was usually the seizure of the offender's goods to the value of the Rate owing, as this extract from the *Leicester Mercury* illustrates. William Pochin, Henry Davis Pochin's father, once had 2½ cwt of cheese impounded from his warehouse for non-payment of such Rates.

1838, apprenticed for five years to Mr. Harris, a chemist and druggist of Gold Street, Northampton. On the completion of that apprenticeship he went to Manchester, where he joined the staff of James Woolley, a well-known and progressive chemist and druggist. His commencing salary was £7 per quarter, an amount that probably included an allowance for board and lodging, for Woolley had a house-keeper who lived on the premises and looked after the requirements of his assistants who "lived in".

Pochin's decision to go to Manchester may have been influenced by an aunt, Mrs. Davis, who lived in the town and appears to have had social or religious connections with the Woolley family, but apart from that there were other reasons why the choice may have been considered a wise one. As the town was the centre of a rapidly growing industrial area with no less than seventy-six chemists and druggists, and thirty-three manufacturing chemists, of varying degree, the opportunities for experience and progress were great for a young man. In addition, there was a branch of the Pharmaceutical Society of Great Britain in the town, and a scheme had been introduced whereby chemists and their assistants could receive further training and attend a course of lectures at the local Infirmary. They also had the use of their own technical library.

Pochin, who undoubtedly reaped great benefit from the training scheme and from his association with James Woolley, remained in Manchester for just under three years, after which, on his twenty-first birthday, he decided to move to Edinburgh, where he took a position in the establishment of Raimes & Co., a firm of druggists with whom Woolley had dealings at the time.   At Raimes', which later became Raimes Clark & Co., the Scottish wholesale druggists, he received a salary of £55 per annum, but stayed with them for only two years after which he apparently went to London, for a notice in the Pharmaceutical Journal in 1847 announced that he had won a Certificate of Merit in the Pharmaceutical Society's Materia Medica Examination held at the London School of Pharmacy.

DISTRIBUTION OF PRIZES TO THE SUCCESSFUL COMPETITORS IN THE CLASS OF MATERIA MEDICA.

The Council having decided that the distribution of prizes which had been awarded in the class of Materia Medica, should take place at the Anniversary Meeting, the Chairman called on Dr. Pereira to report the result of the examination.

Dr. Pereira said he had much pleasure in giving a satisfactory report of the class which had attended the lectures on Materia Medica. A larger number of competitors than usual had presented themselves at the examination, and he could assure the meeting that those to whom he had awarded the prizes and honorary certificates, had most amply merited them. The questions he had drawn up were of a very searching character, and the answers indicated a high degree of proficiency on the part of the pupils, and especially of those to whom the prizes had been awarded. In fact, he had observed throughout the course, that there were a large number of intelligent and well-informed young men among the pupils, whose attention, zeal, and general good conduct, were highly commendable. It must, he thought, be satisfactory to the Society to find, after the heavy expense which had been incurred in establishing a system of education for the rising generation of Chemist and Druggists, that it was the means of developing the talents of so many young men who would reflect credit and honour on the body to which they belonged.

The prizes and honorary certificates were awarded as follows :—

LECTURE PUPIL.

PRIZE ....Mr. William Copney, at Mr. Hawxby's, 37, Berner's-st.

LABORATORY PUPILS.

FIRST PRIZE...............Mr. R. W. Giles, of Clifton.
SECOND PRIZE ....Mr. J. C. Braithwaite, of Bartonsham House, Hereford.

CERTIFICATES OF MERIT.—1. Mr. H. D. Pochin.
2. Mr. R. S. Starkie, 4, Strand.
3. Mr. R. H. Harrison.

The Chairman, in presenting the prizes and honorary certificates, congratulated those who received them on the successful result of their studies, and expressed the satisfaction it had afforded him to hear so favourable an account not only of those who had thus publicly distinguished themselves, but of the pupils generally in the school.

Extract from the *Pharmaceutical Journal*, 1847-48

Pharmaceutical Society of Great Britain
London School of Pharmacy
(Materia Medica Examination)

Following that success it might have been expected that he would have continued with his pharmaceutical career, but instead he seems to have decided that the chemical side of the business offered more scope, and when he rejoined James Woolley in Manchester, in 1848, it was for a nominal salary of £20 per annum plus a share of the profits on the chemicals he sold. Woolley had by that time become interested in heavy chemicals as well as pharmaceuticals and was a partner in the firm of A. P. Halliday & Co., Manufacturing Chemists of Quay Street, Salford, many of whose products found their way to the dyers and bleachers via his chemist's shop in Market Street.

Very soon, Pochin was selling substantial quantities of those chemicals, chiefly acetates and alums, and his knowledge of them and of their uses was such that, when A. P. Halliday was suddenly taken ill, in 1849, James Woolley asked him to take temporary charge of the Company's chemical works in Quay Street. This request was followed shortly afterwards by an offer of a partnership in A. P. Halliday & Co., provided he invested the sum of £600 in the Company. William Pochin agreed to lend his son the money and, on the 21st December, 1849, a Deed of Partnership for seven years was drawn up. It was between Andrew Paton Halliday, James Woolley, and Henry Davis Pochin, for the manufacture of Red Liquor, British Gum, and other such articles as might be agreed upon. To this partnership Halliday apparently contributed the goodwill, James Woolley £1,000, and Pochin £600 with the provision for a further £400 should the business be in need of that sum.

Twelve months after the formation of the new Company, Pochin's father, who had given so much financial help to his son, died, and shortly afterwards the Company appeared in Slaters Directory as Halliday, Pochin & Co. Another change followed almost immediately after when, on the death of A.P. Halliday, the Company became known as Pochin & Woolley.

In 1852, after the death of his father, Pochin married Agnes Heap, the youngest daughter of George Gretton and Hannah Heap of Timperley, Cheshire, and a sister of his late partner

Halliday's wife. She was a lady of slight physique but great determination, and an ardent supporter of the rights of women. Whether Pochin supported his wife's views on that vexed question is not known but he certainly shared her passion for reform, particularly in local government matters, and in 1854, the same year in which his second child Laura Elizabeth was born - a son had been born in 1853 - he was elected a member of the Salford Town Council. During his first year on the Council he was appointed Vice-Chairman of its unromantically named, but vitally important, Lamp and Scavenging Committee, and attended nearly a hundred meetings in connection with Council affairs.

Despite those new commitments he continued with the chemical research he had started when he first joined Halliday & Co., and in 1855 he invented and patented a process for the manufacture of a product that was to become the most profitable part of his business and the basis for his later financial undertakings. The product, which he called Aluminous Cake, was prepared by treating a clay containing various proportions of alumina and silicon with sulphuric acid and was intended for use in the paper-making and dyeing industries, and in the preparation of white leather. The discovery by Perkins of the first aniline dye, in 1856, caused its use in the dyeing industry to be of comparatively short duration but in the process of paper-making it almost entirely displaced, according to Cross and Bevan (the authors of a book on the chemicals used in that trade) the alum crystals then in use.

A year after patenting his Aluminous Cake, Pochin invented and patented another process, this time for the production of improved forms of alumina and silicon compounds for use in dyeing and paper-making. He was an indefatigable researcher and a keen observer of the uses to which the chemicals he sold were being put, and both of these inventions must have come about as a result of his intimate knowledge of those industries.

The successful commercial exploitation of the inventions involved the use of large quantities of material and heavy plant, and he and Woolley soon realised that their premises at Quay Street, Salford, were inadequate for any substantial development of the patents.   In 1855, therefore, they acquired an additional site, with a wharfage on the Rochdale Canal, at Vickers Street, Newton Heath, Manchester.   The site, which covered an area of 3,383 square yards had previously been occupied by another chemical manufacturer, Thos. Kenyon, and contained plant that could be used temporarily until permanent fixtures were erected.   As the partners had also decided to make their own sulphuric acid for use in the manufacture of the Cake, it was necessary for them to build special pyrites or sulphur-ore furnaces for that purpose, and records show that before they did this they took the best possible advice.

Some men would have been satisfied with the bringing of one project to such a conclusion, but not so Pochin, and whilst he had been bound up with all the details necessary for the production of his Aluminous Cake he had somehow found the time to continue with his research on another project. In 1858, in conjunction with a fellow chemist, Edward Hunt, he invented and patented a process for the purification of brown rosin, a substance that had been used in the manufacture of the cheaper yellow soaps since 1845. With the new discovery it became possible, for the first time, for manufacturers to use that substance in the manufacture of the dearer fancy soaps, a considerable step forward!

With the foundations apparently laid for a successful and profitable future, both for himself and the Company, the year 1858 should have been one of the brightest in Pochin's career but, unfortunately, it became one of tragedy and uncertainty. Early in the year his partner, James Woolley, became suddenly ill and despite three operations carried out by a leading Edinburgh surgeon, Professor Syme, he died on 30th January at the comparatively early age of forty-eight.

During Woolley's illness, Pochin's fourth child, Beatrice, who had been born in the previous June, also became ill and entries in his diary vividly illustrate the stress under which he must have lived at the time. They also show the great trust that existed between the two partners, for at one stage in the operations it was Pochin who administered the chloroform at Woolley's special request. The operations were carried out at Woolley's home and appear to have been the first occasion on which the new anaesthetic was used in the North of England.

The reference to a Court case in the diary was concerned with a dispute that had arisen between Pochin and another inventor who claimed to have discovered a product similar to Pochin's Aluminous Cake. There is no record of the case ever having been heard.

Professor James Syme, who was considered one of Europe's leading surgeons, had at one time, along with many members of the medical profession and the clergy, vigorously opposed the use of chloroform when it was first introduced into medical practice by Simpson in 1847. One of Syme's assistants was Joseph Lister (later Lord Lister) who became his son-in-law.

Extracts from Pochin's Diary

Sunday, January 17th.
Mr. Woolley worse... went over to Stockport
to see Dr. Raynor. Afterwards saw Dr.
Harrison. To Mr. Woolley's again at 6. o'clock.
Home in the evening.

Monday, January 18th.
Mr. Woolley still very unwell indeed but better.
Heȳwood Masters went to Bakewell. To Newton
Heath. Saw Mr. Woolley in the evening.

Tuesday, January 19th.
Saw Mr. W. again. A little better. Called to
see Mr. Shipman and ask him to see Mr. Woolley.
Saw Fielden who acknowledged we were the first
to make Aluminous Cake or the article containing
the Silica and he said we ought to win the trial.
Saw Mr. W. in the evening. To Newton Heath in
the morning.

Wednesday, January 20th.
Mr. Woolley's operation performed... last
night Syme arrived from Edinburgh... there
were present Syme, Raynor, Jordan, and
Harrison. He appeared not to be all the time
perfectly under the influence of the chloroform...
they were nearly $1\frac{1}{2}$ hours upstairs. In the
afternoon they found they had not cut into the
uretha but were cutting at the false passage.
They again operated, i.e. Syme and Harrison
but did not give the chloroform and could not
get on. Mr. Woolley screamed very much and
another operation will be necessary in the
morning... poor fellow.

Thursday, January 21st.
I slept at Mr. Woolley's last night... he is very wonderfully well this morning as he wished me to administer the chloroform. I was present at the operation... it is <u>terrible butchery</u>. The operation did not last more than twenty minutes... he was perfectly insensible all the time. All think it successful this time and it appears to be so. Mr. W. is better than expected. I went to Stockport to fetch Dr. Raynor before the operation. In Newton Heath in the afternoon.

Friday, January 22nd.
Dr. Syme left today at 1. o'clock. Mr. W. going on very favourably. Went to Newton Heath... Jeans is going on with the Pyrites Furnaces... bought iron for the stays. In Mr. Woolley's in the evening. Received samples of Aluminous Cake from London that his men told would upset my patent and certainly it looks very like our manufacture but it contains very little or so of Silica and as full of... no fear of that.

Saturday, January 23rd.
To Newton Heath in the evening... to the Commercial to see Aitkens colour mixed. Bleeding has commenced from the wound and Mr. Woolley is not nearly so well.

Sunday, January 24th.
To Mr. Woolley's early... there is not so much bleeding this morning but it has weakened him very much. I have great fears of him. Called upon Mr. Jackson and he gave me a receipt to make some juice of flesh. I took a

little to Mr. Woolley... Mr. Henry came in
the afternoon. He left at $\frac{1}{2}$past 9. o'clock and
went to Mr. Woolley's and slept there.

Monday, January 25th.
  Mr. Woolley is a little more comfortable this
morning. To Newton Heath. Cox was here
from Bristol. He is in a poor way and will I
doubt not shortly fail. To Mr. Woolley's to
sleep. I was going to bed when Mrs. Woolley
came into the room and asked me to sit with her
for a little as she feared Mr. Woolley was very
much worse.

Tuesday, January 26th.
  Mr. Woolley still very ill... I was with him all
day and sat up with him during the night. About
3 or 4. o'clock we called George up as we thought
he could not continue along... he appeared but
to breathe.

Wednesday, January 27th.
  Mr. Woolley sinking... cannot continue long in
this state... if he does not get better soon he
cannot live... in great pain during the night,
evident symptoms of Gastric Fever... poor
man... I am afraid he cannot recover. Dr.
Harrison stayed all night. I sat up with him.

Thursday, January 28th.
  Mr. Woolley appeared better this morning and
even spoke of going to Bath... poor man he
does not know how ill he is... the children
came in to kiss him I could not but feel it was
the last kiss they would give him notwithstanding
he is better. I sat up with him all night... he
has great pain in the knee

Friday, January 29th.
  Mr. Woolley sinking fast... I was with him
  during the day and sat up with him during the
  night... I did not expect him to last through
  the night.   He was more violent than he has
  ever been.   Our baby taken ill last night.

Saturday, January 30th.
  It is now a question of how many hours Mr.
  Woolley can live... I left him in the morning
  for about two hours... he did but just know
  me when I returned.   I continued with him all
  day and he died about a minute after 6. o'clock.
  I closed his eyelids after death.   There were
  present Mrs. Woolley, myself, Mr. Hyde,
  Mr. John Woolley and Miss Johns.   Poor man...
  I lose a friend of no common character.   His
  place will never be supp'd.   Baby no better.

There is no doubt that the death of James
Woolley came as a great shock to Pochin, for
the two men had much in common apart from
their business partnership.   The shock was
heightened, less than a month later, by the
death of his own baby, Beatrice, at the age of
eight months.   She was the second child Pochin
had lost in eighteen months, the other being
Cecil Emerson, a boy born on 10th January, 1856,
who had died eight months later.

CHAPTER II

James Woolley had held the predominant
amount of capital in Pochin and Woolley ever
since the days when it was known as A. P. Halliday
& Co., and when he died Henry Davis Pochin was
faced with the task, not only of financing the
chemical business himself but of paying to
Woolley's Executors the sum of £10,000, the
amount they calculated as being his share of the
business. An arrangement was made whereby
the money could be paid over a period of ten years
and as security for this arrangement, and to help
cover future expenditure on his Aluminous Cake
project, Pochin took out a life policy for £2,000
with the Globe Assurance Company and mortgaged
his business premises for £9,800. He also
relinquished his interest in the rosin process,
selling one third of the patent to J. T. Johnson,
Soap Maker, of Runcorn Gap, near Warrington,
and another third to a Mr. Fehram. The
remaining third, presumably, went to the co-
inventor of the process, Edward Hunt. The
price obtained was £3,000, plus the expenses
incurred in the development of the patent. He

17

Henry Davis Pochin
Founder of Messrs H. D. Pochin & Co. Ltd.

Photograph of engraving by Rajon of a portrait by W. Ouless, R.A., exhibited at the Royal Academy under the title "The Chemist". The experiment shown is the process patented by Mr H. D. Pochin for the clarification of Rosin.

18

always retained a considerable pride in the rosin process, which could have proved lucrative to the Company, and when, in 1874, he had his portrait painted by Ouless, he was shown sitting at his laboratory table behind the apparatus used in the original experiments. The portrait, which was exhibited at the Academy under the title "The Chemist", now hangs in the dining-room at Bodnant Hall.

Having disposed of his interest in the rosin process, and in so doing relieved himself of any immediate financial worry, Pochin was then free to concentrate his efforts on the manufacture of his Aluminous Cake. He had found that the best clay for his purpose came from the china-clay mines of St. Austell, in Cornwall, and was already being used by the Staffordshire pottery makers. It was transported, usually by coastal schooners, to the port of Runcorn in Cheshire,

Pochin's Aluminous Cake, or Alum Cake as it was described in an advertisement in 1865, proved a great success and his Company made rapid progress. In 1863 he opened a new branch at Temple Back, Bristol, and two years later one at Willington Quay, Newcastle-upon-Tyne. As both these sites were close to the sea and the coalfields he was able to get his pyrites, which came usually from Spain, Portugal, Norway or Westphalia, to his works without excessive transport costs.

He had, by this time, been joined by other members of his family and much of the every-day running of the business was left in the hands of his brothers, William and Edward Davis Pochin, though he himself remained in strict control. His great interest in local affairs had continued and he had come to be regarded with respect, and no little apprehension, on the Salford Town Council as an indomitable individualist who spoke his mind freely and made no party alliances. For a short time he was off the Council and when he sought re-election, in 1859, it was as President of the Ratepayers Association. His election manifesto on that occasion reveals something of the uncompromising attitude he adopted towards any matter with which he was not in agreement.

Gentlemen,

I have been requested by a large and influential body of ratepayers to allow myself to be nominated as a Candidate for the honour of representing your interests in the borough council. This request being accompanied by the assurance that I should, if returned, be enabled to render efficient assistance in securing for the Salford district good and economical government, has induced me, after some hesitation, to accept the proffered honour. It is probably known to most of you that as a burgess and rate-payer I have recently taken an active part in opposing, before a Committee of the House of Commons, some of the provisions of the Salford Gas Bill. To this course I was impelled by the gross injustice to the Salford district, and because I failed to see why this poor district should sell an interest in property that had cost upwards of £100,000, and that has been returning a clear net profit of £7,000 per annum, to the districts of Broughton and Pendleton at a valuation of £77,000. This opposition no doubt cost the borough a considerable sum of money. Unless, however, the proceedings of Broughton and Pendleton shall be far different in future to what they have been in the past, I am prepared to compel a much larger legal expenditure than before. Any who have charges to bring against me, or wish to know the reasons which actuate my proceedings, will have

ample opportunity afforded them in the
borough council should I be returned as
your representative. I do not imagine
that you will think it necessary for me
to state my general principles at any
length, my past conduct on the council
is known to you: my wishes are the
same now as they were before: the
motives that then actuated my proceedings
will continue to do so, and if it be your
wish that I should represent you in the
borough council be assured that I will give
my best exertions to secure your interests.

Throughout all his time on the Council Pochin
adopted this rather moralistic but keenly business-
like approach to Local Government.   The Gas
Department must show a profit and at the same time
be aware of its moral duties.   He once said that he
believed the effect of lighting every small tenement
with gas would be to keep the working man at home
during the evenings instead of his going into one of
the many surrounding public houses.

Pochin, who was returned unopposed to the Council, had no great love, at that time, for the districts of Broughton and Pendleton which, though forming part of the Borough under the Salford Extension Act of 1853, had power to levy their own Improvement and Highways Rate and to appoint their own officers. Under the constitution they were entitled to a share of the profits made by the Salford Gas Undertaking and it was his contention that those profits should be used for the improvement of the districts (a Government Report, in 1851, had strongly indicted Pendleton regarding its sanitation and water supply) and not, as had been the case, for the relief of rates. He had felt so strongly about this, before his election, that he had threatened the Salford Council, as the overall authority, with proceedings for the mis-appropriation of the gas profits.

Another matter in which Pochin took a particular interest was that of education, for which there was a growing need in his time. Though a voluntary educational system, run chiefly by the churches and other bodies, existed with Government support, many children, for various reasons, received no education at all while others, sent to work at an early age, never got beyond the elementary stage. To help bridge this immense gap in the system reformers throughout the country had set up Mechanics' Institutes and Working Mens' Clubs where young workers and others could be taught in the evenings. The number of those institutions was, however, limited and they touched only a fraction of the population as Pochin, like others, knew. In the early 1850's he had attempted to form an additional Club in Manchester but the attempt had failed for want of support, but in Salford he and some friends, including the Borough Treasurer, David Chadwick, were more successful and they established the Salford Working Mens' College in Great George Street. The College had eight-hundred students on its books and the subjects taught, between 7. 00 p. m. and 10. 00 p. m. ranged from elementary reading and writing to foreign languages and logic. Established originally for men and boys only, the feminist zeal of Pochin's wife soon broke through the sex barrier and in 1860 she and a Mrs. Plant of Peel Park were teaching classes of girls with the full approval of the College's council, which was composed of both teachers and pupils. The Salford Working Mens' College later ran a school for girls. Pochin referred to the College as doing for working men precisely what Eton and Harrow did for the more fortunate members of society, and that idealistic and rather grandiose outlook was apparent in much of what he did and said. Even in his support for the Salford Free Library, one of the first of its kind to be established in the country, he made a gift of books which were probably far beyond the understanding of the majority of the readers for whom they were intended: "Arte Gymnastica", Count Saxe's "Memoirs", Bellershien's "Fortifications", La Blond's "Engineers (Military)", "Tactics of Oelian", De Bruge's "Castramentation", Sime's "Military Regulator".

His interest in military matters seems to have stemmed from a meeting held in the Salford Town Hall in December, 1859, for the purpose of considering the best means of aiding the formation of a regiment of riflemen for the Borough. There was a large attendance of working men to whom he delivered a speech Churchillian in style. After expressing his pleasure at the way the movement had taken hold of Salford he said he knew there was some opposition but he thought that sprang from a fear lest the rifle movement should result in infusing too generally into the inhabitants a desire for military glory. If that were the case, he said, it would be a disaster, but he believed too much in the intelligence of people for that to happen. He expressed the hope that they would, as Christians, maintain a wholesome hatred of war but, at the same time, be determined to maintain a peace consistent with the honour of the country. Though he hated war, he added amidst cheers, he would be ashamed to live in a street with a man who would not, in the case of a foreign invasion, shoulder his musket, or any other weapon he could lay hands on, and be off by the first train to give them battle. "If to-morrow", he concluded, "a French or any other invader were to land on these shores we should expel him at a terrible loss of good English blood. Let us prepare ourselves. let every man be able to use a rifle with skill and success and we will repel the invader without great loss of good English blood; we will do it economically and cheaply. We will meet them not only with the hearts of lions but we will meet them with the skill of riflemen, and if they come once, they will not come again."

There is no record of Pochin actually joining the rifle corps, though his wife was a member of a committee of Salford ladies formed for the purpose of raising funds for the presentation of silver bugles to each Company of the Salford Regiment.

If the year 1858, with the death of James Woolley and the period of business uncertainty that followed, had been a momentous one for Pochin, the year 1862 proved to be one with more far reaching effects for it saw the passing of the Companies Act of 1862 and the beginning of his career as a financier and industrialist. But before then he had suffered a further personal tragedy by the loss of another child, Bertha Mabel, who had been born on the 20th September, 1859, and had died on the 13th March, 1862. Three months later, however, his second son and last child, Percival Gerald, was born at Oakfield House, Windsor Bridge, Salford. Pochin was then thirty-eight, and out of the six children born to him and his wife during their ten years of married life only three had survived. It says much for his tenacity of purpose that with all the personal tragedy he experienced he continued, not only with his business commitments but with his efforts to make the town in which he lived a better place for its citizens.

Much of Salford's prosperity depended, of course, on the cotton and allied trades and when, during 1862, there was a cotton famine as a result of the American Civil War, the town suffered great distress, many mills being closed down and thousands of people thrown out of work. The distress reached such proportions that a National Appeal for funds was launched and Boards of Guardians were allowed to obtain loans as a mean of meeting the demands upon them. At the peak of the distress it was estimated that the Poor Law Unions and the Committees administering the proceeds of the National Appeal

Fund, which had reached £1,974,200, were affording relief to no less than 496,816 people.

Poor Law Relief, which amounted to about 1/4d per week per person, was augmented whenever possible by a grant from the local Relief Committee in order to bring the total amount received to 3/- per week for a single adult; 5/6d for two adults; 6/6d for two adults with one child, and 7/6d for two adults and two children, with 1/- per week extra for each additional child. In the greater number of cases relief was paid in the form of tokens which the recipient took to a local shopkeeper. The Salford Relief Committee, of which Pochin was an active member, based its scheme of administration on that of Manchester where the districts were divided into wards with four or five visitors to each ward. These visitors investigated each case and reported back to the Committee.

In addition to relief in kind the Committee also tackled the problem of inactivity and engaged rooms, with fires, where men could meet and where, rather optimistically perhaps, it was

"SEWING SCHOOL.— Females desirous of entering a sewing school, must apply at the rooms of the committee, as in the case of an application for relief. If on investigation by the Relief Committee the applicant be deemed eligible, she will receive a ticket of admission, which will entitle her to admission to any school recognised by the committee. Those attending the committee's school must take their places in such class as the superintendent shall direct. The superintendent must keep a register of attendances, and any worker who may be more than half an hour late will be refused admission for that half day. Each worker must take her place in her class at nine o'clock and half past one. As soon as each class is seated, the teacher is to give out the work to each worker in her class. When notice is given to close the school at half past twelve, and at five o'clock, each worker must neatly fold her work, and tie her number to it, and deliver it to her teacher. All broken needles must be given immediately to the teacher, and by her to the superintendent. All pins, needles, and thread must be returned to the teacher as soon as done with. No loud talking permitted, nor any singing, except under the direction of the superintendent. All attendants at the school must obey the directions of the superintendent; and each teacher must keep order in her own class, and if any worker be disobedient she must be reported to the superintendent, who may at her discretion dismiss the disobedient worker, or refer her case to the committee. Any worker may purchase any article, when made, for the value of the materials used therein. She may pay by instalments, but must not take away the article until the whole amount due for it has been paid. If any worker wish to work any particular article for herself, or for any member of her family, she may do so on giving notice to the superintendent, and, when completed, may have the same on payment of the value of the material used therein. Teachers will be selected from applicants who may be competent, and will be paid 10d. per day. Cutters-out will also be selected in like manner, if any competent apply, and will be paid 1s. per day. Workers above 16 years of age will be paid 8d. per day; and those under 16 years of age 6d. per day, inclusive, in all cases, of any allowance made by the guardians of the poor. The school will be open on Mondays, Tuesdays, Wednesdays, Thursdays, and Fridays, from 9 to 12 30, and 1 30 to 5 o'clock.

Rules of the Regent Street Sewing School.
From the *Salford Weekly News,* 16 October 1862.
Pochin helped to raise Funds for the School

hoped that lectures would be arranged. For the girls, a large number of whom were out of work, Sewing Schools were established in which they could be taught sewing and, at the same time, receive payment for the work they did. This arrangement brought about the almost inevitable argument that the earnings of the girls should be offset against relief grants to their families. Pochin vigorously opposed any such action, saying that he would not have asked people to subscribe to the Relief Fund had he thought their subscriptions would have been used for the purpose of relieving the local rates. He said the girls earning the money at the schools were doing so through no fault of their own, they honestly wanted work and what they earned should have no connection with Poor Law Relief.

CHAPTER III

The writer of an obituary notice in the
Journal of the Manchester Literary and
Philosophical Society said of Henry Davis
Pochin, who had been a member of the Society
since 1854, "Many men make money in their
own business but are just as unfortunate when
they engage in other enterprises.   Mr. Pochin
was an exception to that rule being, on the whole,
very fortunate in his speculations."

Pochin was indeed fortunate in that the
period during which his own chemical business
began to make substantial profits coincided with
the passing of the Companies Act of 1862, a
measure that opened the way for fresh capital
investment in many of the leading industries of
the country.   Important groups of capitalists in
Lancashire and Yorkshire took advantage of the
Act to invest their accumulated savings in the
establishments of old private firms who wished
to withdraw from their businesses because of
their financial inability to meet the growing
foreign competition which had come about as a
result of technological and scientific advances.

After the passing of the Act thousands of new companies were 'floated' and the paid up capital of limited companies subsequently increased enormously.

As a result of enemy air activity during the Second World War no figures are available of the profits made by Pochin's chemical business during the 1860's, but they were sufficient to enable him to join a group of Manchester capitalists who had formed themselves into a syndicate for the purpose of floating new companies under the 1862 Act. The syndicate appears to have concentrated its attention chiefly on the engineering and allied industries which had probably been the worst hit by foreign competition and one of its first acquisitions was the Staveley Coal & Iron Company which had been founded in the 18th century and was then in the hands of Richard Barrow. The new Company was floated on the 24th December, 1863, with a capital of £600,000 divided into 6,000 shares of £100 each, and Pochin was appointed its first Chairman with Charles Markham as Managing Director.

An intriguing feature about the original subscribers of that Company was that each of them had strong radical leanings and that three of them, Henry Davis Pochin, Benjamin Whitworth and David Chadwick, ultimately became Liberal Members of Parliament only to suffer the same fate of being unseated following petitions made under the Parliamentary Act of 1868. Benjamin Whitworth was a member of the firm of Ben. Whitworth & Bro. , Fustian Makers, of Manchester, and lived at Fleetwood, though he had a house in Manchester. He was also an importer of timber and one of the largest importers of cotton in the country, owning a considerable number of his own vessels. He was a total abstainer and one of the shrewdest men in business at the time. John Hall, who died in 1887, was a well-known silversmith of King Street, Manchester, and was said to have amassed a large fortune before his retirement to a house situated between Menai Bridge and Beaumaris. He was reputed to have been an exceedingly generous man. David Chadwick, who was Borough Treasurer of Salford when Pochin first joined the Salford Town

Council, was a man with an exceptional talent for figures and statistics. He published several pamphlets on the economics of life insurance which attracted much attention and had been induced to leave the Council, in 1860, to enter the service of the Globe Insurance Company as their local agent. Soon after the passing of the 1862 Act he found new scope for his activities and founded the Manchester syndicate of investors. Chadwick achieved a remarkable success and became a recognised power in the financial and commercial world. In 1874, when one of the two Liberal Members of Parliament for Macclesfield, he presented the town with a commodious free library. He was an Honorary Secretary and President of the Manchester Statistical Society, and wrote for it a history of rates of wages in Lancashire which covered 200 trades for 20 years.

Following the conversion of the Staveley Coal & Iron Company the syndicate next turned its attention to John Brown & Co., of Sheffield, and on 3rd March, 1864, an agreement was made between John Brown, John Devonshire Ellis and William Bragge, called the Vendors, of Sheffield, and Charles Patrick Stewart and John Cheetham of the County of Cheshire, Benjamin Whitworth, Henry Davis Pochin and James Holden, all of the City of Manchester, called the Promoters, for the promotion of a new Company to be called John Brown & Co. The nominal capital of the new Company was fixed at £1,000,000, divided into 10,000 shares of £100 each. Although John Brown, who later became Sir John Brown, remained Chairman of the newly formed Company, Henry Davis Pochin, with his financial knowledge, was considered to be the outstanding figure on the new Board of Directors, and the instigator of a move that resulted in Charles Patrick Stewart, a Manchester engineer, becoming both a Director and a substantial shareholder of the new Company. Amongst the original subscribers, the name of Edward Ryley Langworthy appears for the first time as a member of the Manchester syndicate and it is interesting to observe that he, like Pochin and Chadwick, had close connections with the Salford Town Council, and had been Mayor of the Town from 1848 to 1851.

He was a Trustee of the Manchester Grammar

School, to which he donated £20,000, and a founder of the Salford Free Library. He gave the Library £6,000 and also left £10,000 to build a wing to the Peel Park Museum, Salford, which was opened in 1878. A benefactor of Owen's College to the extent of £10,000, his Personality was sworn under £1,200,000 after his death in 1874.

On 8th September, 1864, the Manchester syndicate purchased the Sheepbridge Ironworks which had been established in 1856 by Fowler and Hankey, and floated it as a limited liability Company with a nominal capital of £500,000 divided into 5,000 shares of £100 each. By the end of the year the group had gained sufficient confidence and support to undertake the conversion of Bolckow Vaughan & Co., the Ironmasters, of Middlesbrough, and the founders, in 1841, of the Cleveland iron industry. The new Company was registered on 19th November, 1864, with a nominal capital of no less than £2,500,000, divided into 25,000 shares of £100 each. Pochin, who had taken out two hundred of the original shares, ultimately became Chairman of the Company.

There is no further evidence, after the acquisition of Bolckow Vaughan & Co., of the activities of the Manchester syndicate which by then had been responsible for the flotation of Companies with a total nominal capital of £4,600,000, but in 1865 the two most influential members of the syndicate, Pochin and Chadwick, became heavily involved in a new venture, the conversion into a Public Company of Palmers Shipbuilding and Iron Company. In the Memorandum of the new Company, Chadwick's address, for the first time, is given as being in London, where he had established himself as a financial agent, and although the issue attracted support from all over the country, all the original shareholders came either from London or Tyneside, where Pochin had considerable influence. The nominal capital of this Company was £2,000,000, divided into 40,000 shares, of which Pochin and Chadwick each held 1,000. Pochin was elected Vice-Chairman of the new Company.

CHAPTER IV

It was in 1865, following his debut as a Company promoter, that Henry Davis Pochin

made his first incursion into national politics.
Previous to then there is no record of his having
appeared on any political platform, though he was
closely associated with the so-called Manchester
School which included such radicals as John Bright
and Richard Cobden. The invitation to stand as a
Liberal candidate for the County Borough of
Stafford came late as a consequence of the sudden
withdrawal, on account of ill health, of the official
candidate, and with little more than twelve days in
which to canvas the borough he was compelled to
rely almost entirely on the arrangements already
made by his predecessor. A further difficulty
arose when he arrived at Stafford for there he
found that his nomination had not been unanimous,
and it was not until four days before the poll that
matters were straightened out and he was free to
move about without restriction. He lost the
election, which cost him upwards of £3,000, by
598 votes to his opponent's Col. Meller's, 658.
The contest was not a particularly happy one from
many points of view, as later events proved, but
that was hardly apparent from the speeches
delivered at a dinner he gave to his committee

and friends on 2nd August. The dinner, which took place at the Swan Hotel, Stafford, was described by a Salford paper as having been "sumptuous". It was attended by upwards of eighty guests, including George Woolley, the son of his former partner, and the Mayor of Salford, who announced in his speech that Pochin had already been pointed out as the most fitting man to sustain the civic honour of his borough during the coming municipal year.

In proposing the toast "The town and trade of Stafford" Pochin begged the assembly to believe him when he said he proposed it with his whole being and with the best feelings. It was impossible, he said, for any human being to have come into a town like theirs, a perfect stranger, and receive the kind of treatment which he had, without feeling a lively interest in its prosperity.

Later, in what an apparently exhausted reporter summarised as a "lengthy speech" in reply to the toast "The health of Mr. Alderman Pochin" the candidate said he had come to Stafford with the desire of serving the Liberal cause. He was quite sure that object was far more to be desired than the attainment of a seat in the House of Commons. To him it was a gain to be sent back to his business, but if he had been returned to Parliament he should have done the best he could to serve the common cause. He was not going to be idle, however, because he was not in Parliament and he hoped those present at the dinner would not be idle. "Hold your principles", he said, "as men and if you think those principles worth fighting for on the day of an election, they are worth fighting for every day." Pochin said he considered himself highly placed that afternoon because he had united the Liberals of Stafford. They must, however, get the best man they could and be united at the next election. He did not ask, he concluded amidst cries of "it will" that that man should be himself and he wished it to be clearly and distinctly understood that no man was there that afternoon because he wished him to vote for him at the next election — he freed everyone from such an obligation. Following this post-election dinner it was decided by the Liberals of Stafford that a testimonial should be made to Pochin for his efforts on their behalf and in October they, in their turn, entertained him to a dinner, after which a procession was formed, headed by the volunteer band, to the Market Hall where nearly 800 people sat down to tea.   Afterwards, a presentation was made to Pochin and his wife of a tea and coffee set and a silver kettle, valued altogether, the paper said, at £180.

Undaunted by his defeat at Stafford, Pochin, as he had promised his supporters at the dinner given in his honour, began to take a more active part in politics and in March 1866 he attended a Reform Demonstration in Salford.   True to his nature he voiced his difference of opinion with some of his colleagues on the platform saying that he could not go as far as them on the matter of reform but he did, in the strictest honesty, wish for a much larger amount of political power to be extended to the masses of the people.   He added that he would be equally honest in saying that he did not want the existing unfranchised class to "swamp" the present holders of political power.   He did not think that was desirable. "On the other hand", he concluded, "the present holders of power should not swamp the other classes to their own advantage. "

Following the Reform Demonstration, Pochin published a booklet, "A Plan for Parliamentary Reform", in which he set down his solution to the vexed problem of the extension of the franchise. The problem was occupying the attention of both the Liberal and Conservative parties and also of the trade unions who were demanding a greater say in the way in which public money was being spent and in legislation that concerned them. There was general agreement on the need for reform but both the major political parties were afraid of making too drastic a change for fear of losing power, as Pochin's "Plan" illustrates. His solution, as published in his booklet, was ingenious: two separate Registers, and two types of candidate, one to represent voters paying £10 or over in rates - the existing qualification for voting - and another to represent those paying less. By this means, and by some rearrangement of constituencies, he estimated that it would be possible for 58 Members of Parliament, out of a House of 658, to be elected by the working classes. Thus, he said, the voice of labour would be heard and listened to on all subjects that concerned them without any danger to the existing balance of power.

As predicted by the then Mayor at the post-election dinner in Stafford in 1865, Pochin was elected Mayor of Salford in 1866, after twelve years service on the Town Council. There is no doubt that he deeply appreciated the honour conferred upon him and was greatly touched by the unexpected show of unanimity over his election. As he himself said, it had been his misfortune often to differ with the opinions of those he so much esteemed and, at one time or another, to have been at variance with every member on the Council.

In his inaugural speech he referred to one matter in particular about which he had been especially concerned during the whole of his time on the Council, the notoriously high death-rate of the Town. In 1866 it stood at about 28.5 per thousand, one of the highest in the Kingdom, and in some districts of the Town it was as high as 50 or 60 per thousand. That sad

Mayor of Salford 1866-68
Pochin, accompanied by his wife, wearing the
regalia, a robe of blue satin and a sword of
office, that he "invented" for his position as
Mayor.

state of affairs he attributed to bad sanitation and overcrowding, for Salford, like many other towns in the North of England, had not recovered from the effects of an earlier industrialism that, among other things, had left hundreds of acres of its land covered with hastily built and badly constructed houses, streets and courts, for which no adequate paving, drainage, sewerage or lighting had been provided.

Pochin made a good Mayor and enjoyed the position. He was deeply conscious of the dignity of the office of first citizen and during his term of mayoralty he 'invented' a mayoral robe in blue satin together with a sword of office, both of which, unfortunately, have been lost. A large loving cup of classical design, beautifully mounted in gold and emblazoned with the Borough arms and the motto "Drink and be for ever friends", that he presented to the town on the termination of his mayoralty, still stands, however, amongst the municipal plate in the Town Hall at Salford.

Though Pochin's position as Mayor imposed upon him a certain amount of restraint, he had said himself that it would in future be his duty to

guide rather than attempt to enforce decisions,
it also provided him with opportunities for acting
more directly in matters affecting the community.
One such opportunity presented itself in 1866,
when a great flood partially inundated the town
covering four hundred acres of land near the
River Irwell with water one to seven feet deep.
Nearly three thousand houses and sixteen
thousand people were affected, and fifty factories
closed down. Pochin was soon active with relief
measures, and Charles P. Hampson in his book
"Salford through the Ages" describes how, with
the street lamps out of action, rescue parties in
carts and boats worked under his direction with
the aid of torches, and succeeded in rescuing
seven hundred people from their wrecked homes.
He was sensitive to the need for giving help in other
directions during the flood, particularly to the small
shop-keepers who had lost all their stock, and to the
occupiers of five hundred cellar dwellings, and he
immediately drew up plans for their financial relief.

A further opportunity for his organising
ability came in 1867 on the occasion of the Fenian
murder, when a police sergeant was killed. The

persons found guilty of the offence were
awaiting execution in the New Bailey Prison,
Salford, close to Pochin's Quay Street Works,
and as the day of the execution approached
elaborate precautions were taken to prevent
trouble.   Barricades up to twelve feet high
were erected in the streets near the prison and
upwards of 2, 000 special constables were sworn
in at the Town Hall.   Fortunately, the day
passed without incident and Pochin was highly
congratulated on his handling of a situation that
might have had serious results.

Towards the end of his term of office as
Mayor, some of the causes he had consistently
supported during his time on the Council began
to bear fruit and active steps were being taken
to improve the town.   In June 1867, the Council
introduced a new Bye Law to prevent overcrowding, over which the Sanitary Committee at
the time had no control, and during the debate
on the subject it was revealed that in one area
alone as many as 800 people were living to the
acre, and that in 41 dwellings there were 96
sleeping apartments occupied by 522 persons,

Silver Cup presented by Pochin to the Salford Town Council on the termination of his Mayoralty in 1868

an average of $5\frac{1}{2}$ persons to one bedroom.

With all his success and all his efforts, however, Pochin seems to have been constantly dogged by personal tragedy and it was during his term of office as Mayor of Salford, and whilst living at Broughton Old Hall, Salford, that he lost his eldest son, Walter, in 1867. The boy had been on holiday from school when he was taken ill with peritonitis, in all probability appendicitis, and died at the age of fourteen years.

CHAPTER V

Following his unsuccessful attempt to win Stafford in 1865, Pochin was again approached by the Liberal party to stand for that constituency in the General Election of 1868. With memories of the previous election evidently in mind he accepted the invitation but only on the distinct understanding that the forthcoming election should be conducted on 'perfectly pure principles' as he put it. To this end, and to ensure that he did not become involved in expenses such as in 1865, he appointed an agent from outside the constituency to look after his election expenditure whilst at the same time retaining the services of John Follows, a master wood turner, as his general agent. The constituency, under the new Act of 1868, which had added 938,000 new names to the Register, now returned two Members, and Follows was also the agent for the second Liberal candidate, Mr. Chawney.

The election, which was a noisy one and was later to become the subject of an Enquiry, resulted in a win for Pochin who headed the poll with 1,189 votes against the Conservative's (Col. Meller) 1,124 and the second Liberal's 1,107. On the 20th February, 1869, the two Members entered Parliament, and on the 12th of March Henry Davis Pochin made what appears to have been his maiden speech. It was made on a motion of Lord Cecil's urging the Government to take action on the "widespread and reprehensible practices of using false weights and measures and adulterating foods, drinks and drugs, a subject on which, as a chemist, he was well able to speak. He made three further speeches in Parliament before, in May 1869, being summoned along with the other Member for

Stafford to appear before a Court of Enquiry to answer charges relating to the 1868 election, a petition having been lodged against them with regard to certain incidents alleged to have taken place during the election campaign. The charge against Meller was one of bribery and against Poçhin one of intimidation.

Three such Courts had been established under the Act of 1868 to deal with petitions that would formerly have been heard by a House of Commons Committee. They were presided over by a Judge who, sitting without a jury, had the power to unseat a Member if he found sufficient evidence of undue influence having been exerted by him or his agent during an election campaign. Undue influence, in the form of bribery, corruption or intimidation had been a feature of British elections ever since the passing of an Act of 1832 but for various reasons no serious attempt had been made to eradicate the practice until 1868.

Thirty-five petitions were presented after the General Election of 1868, a number substantially below that of the previous election

STAFFORD BOROUGH ELECTION.

[Received 27 May 1869.]

THE PARLIAMENTARY ELECTIONS ACT, 1868.

COURT for the Trial of an Election Petition for the Borough of Stafford, in the County of Stafford, between Joseph Wile and Thomas Smallman, Petitioners; and Henry Davis Pochin, Respondent.

To the Right Honourable the Speaker.

Sir,   15 May 1869.
I HEREBY certify that at the trial of the above election petition, I determined that Henry Davis Pochin, Esquire, the Member whose return and election is complained of, was not duly returned and elected, and that the election was void.

And, in compliance with the directions of "The Parliamentary Elections Act, 1868," section 11, I report,—

(A.) That no corrupt practice has been proved to have been committed by, or with the knowledge or consent of, any candidate at the said election.

(B.) That John Fallows, an agent for Mr. Pochin, was proved at the trial to be guilty of undue influence by inciting a riotous mob to intimidate persons in order to induce them to refrain from voting.

(C.) That there is not reason to believe that corrupt practices have extensively prevailed at the election to which this petition relates.

COLIN BLACKBURN,
Election Judge.

in 1865, which, according to the "Times" had been the most corrupt in the history of the country. It was one to which the Judges and Counsel in the new Courts of Enquiry frequently referred.

Mr. Justice Blackburn heard the petitions against Meller and Pochin and it was established early in the trial that the Borough of Stafford had been no exception to the rule of extensive corruption which prevailed at the 1865 election. It was disclosed that at that election Col. Meller's election expenses for a poll of a little over one-thousand had been returned at £1,300 whereas, it was admitted, they had exceeded £5,000. Whether the additional £3,700 had been paid in the way of corruption, by paying £5 or £10 for a vote, or whether it was all spent by pretending to pay men for services they had not performed, was not established.

During this part of the trial T.A. Readwin, Pochin's financial agent, was cross-examined at length with regard to the expenditure that had passed through his hands at the 1868 election, especially in public houses, and vouchers were produced which showed that one bill for £23 had been received from the Swan Hotel on the morning of November 16th. He said he was inclined to believe that all the things charged for on the bill were not supplied but he had paid for them. He added that there were fifteen clerks at breakfast that morning, but when the Judge asked him if he would have given them champagne he replied "No". Further questioned, Readwin said some of the bills were made out in a very odd way and there was no check on the drinking and eating which went on practically all day. There were plenty of good smokers amongst Mr. Pochin's friends and there was nothing to prevent them getting cigars in the witness's name. Some of Mr. Pochin's friends could also drink considerably. In one bill, sent in by the landlord of the Dolphin Hotel, he said, there was a charge for a large number of cigars and several dozen bottles of sherry which, he supposed, were consumed in the committee-room. Readwin also said that a number of persons from Manchester, who said they were Mr. Pochin's friends, fastened themselves upon him at the Swan Hotel and amongst the bills he received from there was one from a Liverpool tobacconist for £4. 10. 0. for three boxes of cigars. He added that he himself was not a smoker.

Pochin, who was next examined, said that during his unsuccessful canvas of the Borough in 1865 he attained great experience as to the way in which elections were managed there, and when he consented to stand again, in 1868, that experience was fully in mind. He received a distinct assurance from the Liberal Party that the election should be conducted on pure principles and he adopted a system which he thought would effectively prevent any improper expenditure, but it broke down in consequence of the illness and exhaustion of Mr. Readwin. Any person, he said, who expended a shilling improperly on his behalf would have his hottest displeasure. He added that during the 1865 election he had been approached on the day of the election by a man who said "What are you paying?" He replied "Nothing" and asked the man who he was voting for. The man replied "I don't care a d... who, I shall vote for the best payer." Witness said he told him he was a disgusting brute. Pochin said the 1865 election had been conducted in a different way to the one in 1868 and when asked, "Do you mean there was a great deal of corruption?", he replied that he had paid out almost £3,200 at the election and £100 afterwards in subscriptions to Odd Fellows' Societies and the like. He said that the money had been spent in a way he would not allow it to be spent again. It was, however, quite legal. When asked by the Judge how much was spent in 1865 in a manner he would prohibit in 1868, he said "Oh! about a couple of thousand pounds." He continued, he came late into the Borough on that occasion and found that money had been paid for the use of nearly every public house in Stafford as committee rooms and that there was an arrangement whereby every person who worked on the Liberal Party Committee was compensated. There was also another account for refreshments.

When Follows, Pochins' general agent, was cross-examined about the 1865 election he said there were a great number of committees in that year and all members of those bodies, some of whom had been so from May to polling day in

November were paid for their services. He said the total amount paid to the committees was a little over £1,900. In addition to those payments he usually sent gifts consisting of coals, blankets and half-sovereigns to the Member's supporters at Christmas, and that came to about £720. There were also gifts to the poor, and those were not limited to voters. Follows said that he was not aware that any Christmas gifts were given on behalf of Mr. Pochin and, in fact, when he went round to canvas for that gentleman, the poor people regretted the previous Member's going away.

The charge against Pochin, however, was one of intimidation which the petitioners, Joseph Wile and Thomas Smallman, alleged had taken place during the 1868 election. Witnesses for the petitioners gave vivid descriptions of what they alleged took place, particularly on the day of the poll when a policeman said a mob of two-hundred people paraded the town and broke windows. The chaplain of the local jail, in giving evidence, said that on one occasion the reins of his horse had been cut and he had been dragged to the ground and seriously injured. A chemist's assistant stated that a mob, led by Follows, had entered his master's shop and smashed all the windows, whilst another witness alleged that on going to his work at half-past seven in the morning, carrying some documents belonging to his trade, a number of men had surrounded him and insisted that he was bribing. They seized hold of him and took his papers away and then, having satisfied themselves that they were not bribery papers, they gave them back to him and dismissed him, saying that if he dared to vote for Col. Meller they would break his neck.

The Enquiry, which aroused great interest and caused special editions of the local paper to be published, continued with much conflicting evidence being given on both sides until May 15th, when Mr. Justice Blackburn gave his summing up. He took the case of Meller first and said he found the case of bribery proved and that the alleged incidents in public houses had taken place, and that Meller's agent, Arrowsmith, had formed a committee that kept a record of those who had voted in order to reward them for their support.

Because of this, the Judge said he would have to unseat Col. Meller, although he did not think the Member "understood then or understood now how his money had been spent." He added that he believed it was due to Mr. Pochin's having taken his expenditure out of the hands of the old corrupt agents and putting it into the hands of a stranger to the town, that extensive corrupt practices had not taken place during the 1868 election.

Turning to the charge of intimidation against Pochin, Mr. Justice Blackburn said he had come to the conclusion that the incidents complained of had arisen primarily as a result of the vigilance committee founded by his agent, Follows, who had set it up with the idea of discovering corrupt practices on the other side. Originally, it had been intended that this committee of seven named men should sit and receive reports from a band of twenty or thirty non-electors employed as scouts. Unfortunately, the scheme had got out of hand and the scouts were joined by others who paraded the town and invaded the opposing committee-rooms and then reported back to Follows' committee. Having refreshed themselves with food and drink they then went forth on further expeditions of discovery. The Judge said he could understand Follows employing one or two spies, but to let loose such a large crowd was asking for trouble. Nevertheless, he added he did not find sufficient evidence on that ground to render the election void. What did trouble him, was an alleged goad to violence made in a speech by Follows following a case of suspected bribery which had been reported to him. He had to decide whether the report of the speech, which Follows did not deny, was accurate, and he had come to the conclusion that it was and that it was an exhortation to do that which afterwards was done by the mob.

The Judge said he was very sorry indeed to come to that conclusion and to turn Mr. Pochin out for he believed he had honestly endeavoured to make the election pure and to purify the Borough, but it was one of those cases in which gentlemen must learn to take care when they chose their agents, to choose those who could be trusted to avoid, not only bribery and corruption, but also violence and intimidation.

CHAPTER VI

The whole of Henry Davis Pochin's life, from his first going to Manchester in 1843 to his emergence as a company promoter in the 1860's, has so much the appearance of a carefully conceived and carried out plan that a seemingly sudden decision to leave Salford in 1870 and to take up residence at Barn Elms, near London, seems to require an explanation. Yet none can be given with certainty, though later events suggest that it may have been taken because of a desire to be nearer the centre of political life and also of engaging himself more fully in financial matters along with David Chadwick, his Manchester colleague, who was then installed in the Metropolis as a financial agent. The move could possibly have been rendered more attractive by the opportunity it offered for increased social and cultural activities, for both Pochin and his wife were fond of intellectual company and had been noted for their lavish hospitality at Broughton Old Hall, Salford. In addition to those possible explanations for the move lies the noticeable fact that, as Pochin's public and financial career

From a painting by an unknown artist

Broughton Old Hall
(by courtesy of Salford Art Gallery)

Photo: F. Hey

developed so did his taste for property, particularly in the form of larger and more commodious houses with large gardens. Starting his career in a comparatively small house he had moved to a larger one at Windsor Bridge, Salford, and then as his business had grown and he had become first a Councillor and then a Mayor of the Town, he had taken up residence at Broughton Old Hall, a splendid old mansion which stood in grounds sufficiently large to be later turned into a public park. Finally, in 1870, when he had really established himself financially, came the move to Barn Elms. Barn Elms was an old manor house, once connected with the famous Kit Kat Club, that had formerly been the home of Sir Francis Walsingham. During the 1580's Queen Elizabeth the First and her entire Court were three times accommodated there and the Earl of Essex, who much to the Queen's displeasure had secretly married the daughter of Sir Francis, had also lived there from time to time. In 1750 the lease of Barn Elms was conveyed to Sir Richard Hoare and the house was retained in the family until 1827 when a suspension bridge was erected from Barnes to Hammersmith, and the company that

Barn Elms. Surrey.

The seat of The Right Hon. Sir Lancelot Shadwell, Knight, Vice Chancellor of England.

By whom this plate was Presented.

T.Allom.

H.Griffiths.

Photograph by kind permission of the Wandsworth History Society

Vice-Chancellor Shadwell, who died at Barn Elms in 1850, used to bathe every morning, both winter and summer, in the two-acre pond at the rear of the house.

undertook the work bought the estate of Barn Elms and built a road across it. The house itself, which had been greatly restored by the Hoare family, was then acquired by Sir Thomas Edward Colebrook who granted a sublease to Pochin in 1870.

It was while Pochin was living at Barn Elms that he got in touch with Guiseppe Garibaldi, the famous Italian patriot who, in 1848, at the head of a force of 3,000 volunteers had kept an army of 20,000 French at bay for nearly three months. Pochin and his wife were friends and neighbours of Mrs. Chambers, of Putney House, a lady who for many years had been connected with Garibaldi's household, and it was through her that they learned of the involvement of the General's son in some financial losses in England. Garibaldi, who despite his many triumphs was a poor man, was anxious to retrieve the position without discredit to his son and agreed to accept a loan from Pochin of £5,000. This was arranged through Ashurst, Mason and Crisp, the well-known London solicitors, and although Garibaldi offered the Sword of Honour, presented to him by the Italian people, as a security for the loan, this was refused, Pochin preferring instead to trust to the General's promise to repay.

Later, Garibaldi began negotiations for the sale of his memoirs as a means of raising money and also consented, after some persuasion, to accept a pension from his countrymen. With some of the money he received from these sources he was able to repay the loan and, grateful for the kindness shown to him, he presented Pochin with a flock of black and white sheep, said to be Neopolitan, which grazed for many years in the park at Barn Elms. In the same year that he arranged the loan to Garibaldi, Pochin tried to obtain a freehold interest in Barn Elms, but Sir Thomas Colebrook would not accept his offer of £57,000 for the property and after protracted negotiations the attempt was finally called off, much to his disappointment.

It was from Barn Elms that Pochin made what appears to have been his last venture into Company promotion, when he joined a group of financiers, including Benjamin Whitworth, for the purpose of purchasing and turning into a Public Company the Tredegar Ironworks, which had been founded at the end of the 18th century by Samuel Homfray and W. Forman. The new

Photograph by kind permission of the Wandsworth History Society

Barn Elms as it appeared in 1880. Pochin leased the house from 1870 to 1884. It was occupied by the Ranelagh Club from 1894 to 1939. Requisitioned during World War II it was subsequently acquired by the Surrey County Council who demolished it after a fire in 1954.

Company was named the Tredegar Iron & Coal Company, and it had a nominal capital of £1,250,000, divided into 20,000 shares of £50 each, called "A" shares, and 10,000 shares of £25 each, called "B" shares. Soon after its incorporation the new Company began the re-organisation of the Mine and the Ironworks and when, some six years later, the new Pochin Pits were commenced it was Pochin who cut the first sod. He always took a particular interest in this Company, in which he held 2,000 "A" shares, and several members of his family became share-holders. Ultimately his son-in-law, Charles McLaren, became Chairman of the Company.

CHAPTER VII

Never at a loss for words in his speeches, Pochin could be tantalisingly terse in his diary and an entry on 11th July 1874 which reads "Went to Bodnod" hardly prepares the reader for a subsequent one on 27th October which states "Bought Bodnod for £62,500." Bodnod was an estate of some sixty acres near Conway in North Wales and, as in the case of his previous decision to leave Salford for London in 1870, there appears to be no definite explanation for the move to Wales, though as early as 1871 he had bought Haulfre, a leasehold property which stood on the Great Orme's head, no great distance from Bodnod. Possibly his failure to acquire Barn Elms, coupled with a defeat he had just suffered in a bye-election at Monmouth, finally convinced him that the life of a landlord in the Principality, combined with his many business interests, had as much to offer as a life in London and a seat in the House of Commons. The decision must have been a difficult one to make for he was then only fifty years of age and still possessed of an ambition for political reform.

Though he bought Bodnod in 1874, the name of which he changed to Bodnant, thus reverting to the description of the estate in Lloyd's Parochial Queries of 1699, Pochin continued to live at Barn Elms while extensive alterations were being carried out at his new home. By 1876 these had reached such a stage that he was able to move in on 30th August, and in the following November he and his wife received a visit from John Bright who noted in his Diary "To Bodnant to luncheon with Mr. & Mrs. Pochin - a grand mansion being built with much money expended."

Bright's visit may have had some connection with the recently announced engagement of his nephew, Charles Benjamin Bright McLaren, to Pochin's daughter, Laura Elizabeth, but apart from that Pochin and Bright had long been associated with each other and it may not have been a coincidence that in the ill-fated 1868 election at Stafford, Pochin's financial agent should have been Readwin, a former partner of Bright's in an abortive gold mine venture. Bright recorded in his Diary on 31st March 1862, that arrangements had been made for securing a sette or piece of ground near Dolgelly for the purpose of extracting gold from quartz and that he and four others held one half of the shares and Readwin the other half. Five years later, on February 9th 1867, he recorded that Readwin had called to see him and that as a result of that visit he (Bright) had transferred to him all his shares in the Dochan Gold Mine, in which he said "We have lost a large sum and gained some experience." It is interesting to note that Readwin, at the Court of Enquiry following the 1868 election, was described as a minin engineer and patent medicine salesman – a strange mixture of professions! He had also been connected with the "Morning Star" newspaper.

The wedding of Laura Pochin and Charles McLaren, who were both Quakers, took place at the Westminster Meeting the year after Bright's visit to Bodnant and he was present at the breakfast which was held at Barn Elms. For many years after, the names of the bride and bridegroom frequently appear in Bright's Diary. Pochin put Barn Elms into the possession of his daughter in 1880 but he continued to stay there whenever he was in London, and to look after the garden. When the tenancy of the house expired he bought for her No. 22 (later 45) Harrington Gardens into which she and her family moved in 1884.

Bodnant Gardens
Waterfall and dell where Pochin laid out the walks to his own design.

CHAPTER VIII

Meanwhile, when the alterations to the house at Bodnant had been completed, Pochin turned his attention to the grounds and completely re-planned the gardens in conjunction with Mr. Milner, a well-known landscape gardener. He divided them into two parts with a vast lawn sloping down from the house to the valley as a focal point. On the lawn he retained groups of indigenous trees planted in the eighteenth century, but added two cedars, one of which, from North Africa, bore a blue foliage. He laid out to his own design the Pinetum, the extension of the Lily Pond and the walks in the Yew Dell, and it is said that his superintendance of the construction of the rock work at the edges of the streams in the lower garden was as expert as that of Milner's foreman himself. Whether he himself actually utilised the sixteenth century mill-race that ran through the garden is not known, but at one period it was being used for its old purpose of grinding flour, before it finally drove the Bodnant saw-mill. Like many men who design and plant their gardens late in life, Pochin never saw the full fruition of his work which, nevertheless, gave him great pleasure and satisfaction.

In addition to his interest in the gardens at Bodnant, Pochin, who was a keen agriculturalist as well as a horticulturalist, also improved farms and farm buildings on the Estate and built, or re-built, nearly thirty cottages. As his interest in agriculture developed he looked further afield for fresh opportunities and in 1877, after a visit with his wife, daughter and son-in-law, he bought some property at Golden Grove which lay in a belt of farmland between the Clwydian Hills and the sea in North Wales. The following year he purchased Henfryn in the same district and with it two flour-grinding mills, the Grove Mill and the Marian Mill, both of which received their motive power from the water that came from an inexhaustible well on the estate, Fynnon Asaph. After working the gigantic water-wheels of the Mills the water from this well cascaded over the rocks to form the famous Dyserth Falls.

Following his purchase of Henfryn, Pochin continued to acquire more property in the district,

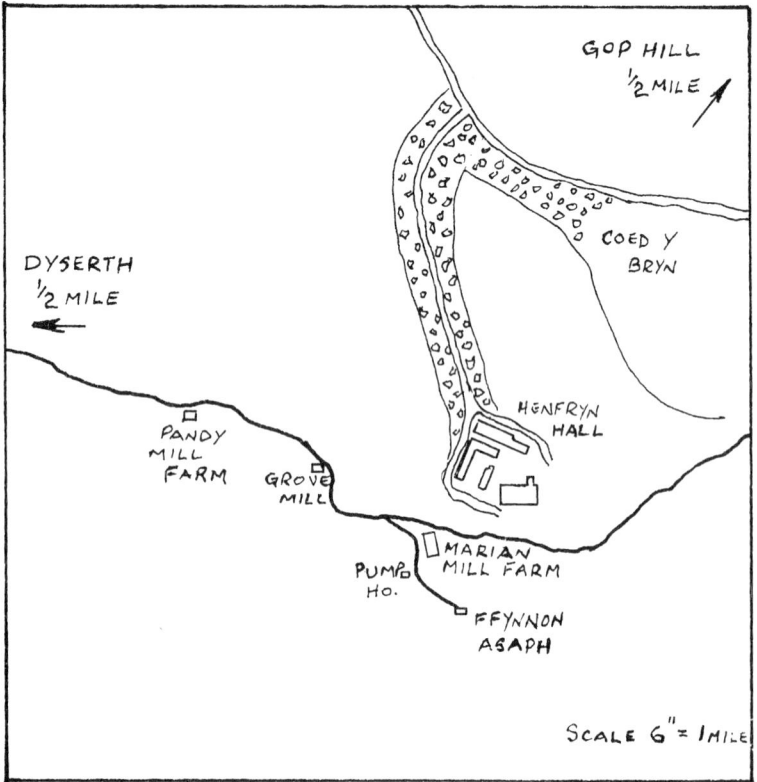

GOP HILL
½ MILE

COED Y
BRYN

DYSERTH
½ MILE

HENFRYN
HALL

PANDY
MILL
FARM

GROVE
MILL

MARIAN
MILL FARM

PUMP
HO.

FFYNNON
ASAPH

SCALE 6" = 1 MILE

(F. HET)

HENFRYN ESTATE SHOWING TWO
FLOUR MILLS.

FROM A 1920 MAP.

buying up farms as they became vacant at Gwaenysgor, Meliden, Newmarket and Llanasa. One of his largest single acquisitions was that of the Nant Estate on the Meliden-Prestatyn border. The estate covered nearly four hundred acres and included, in addition to farms and houses, the Nant Hall which was then in the possession of Mr. Dixon, a gentleman farmer. When, in 1885, he bought the foreshore at Prestatyn from the Ecclesiastical Commissioners he had completed the purchase of an almost continuous stretch of country from the hills to the sea, at a point that was practically the nearest part of the North Wales coast easily accessible by train, and at the same time attractive to North of England visitors. Before he bought the Nant Estate he had obtained a Provisional Order to extract and convey water from his Fynnon Asaph well to Prestatyn and he subsequently did this by means of gravitation, the water being conveyed through pipes that ran along the High Street where it could be obtained by pressing buttons situated at various points. For supplying the water to places above the level of the well, he installed a pumping engine at Henfryn.

Prestatyn at the beginning of the Century.
High Street, looking up to hills, Bethel on right.

Not content with supplying Prestatyn with water,
Pochin also supplied it with gas from his own gas-
works which he constructed at the end of High Street,
and then he turned his attention to the development
of his property within the town's boundaries. He
first constructed a road, the Nant Hall road, across
his Nant Estate, and then proceeded to deal with the
adjoining foreshore which was separated from the
Estate by the Chester-Holyhead railway line. The
foreshore, part of which had once been cultivated
commercially for asparagus by the Rev. Frank
Jewel and his two sons, was subject to flooding, the
danger coming from a narrow sea inlet that led into
a gutter that had been specially built to receive
drainage water from the surrounding high ground.
With a strong North wind and a high tide, the sea
water would sometimes rush up the inlet into the
gutter where it met the land water with disastrous
results, except for the local schoolboys who seized
the opportunity to play truant in order to make
profit from the sale of numerous dead rabbits
washed out of their burrows in the Warren.

To stop this flooding, and to make the land fit
for commercial development, Pochin constructed

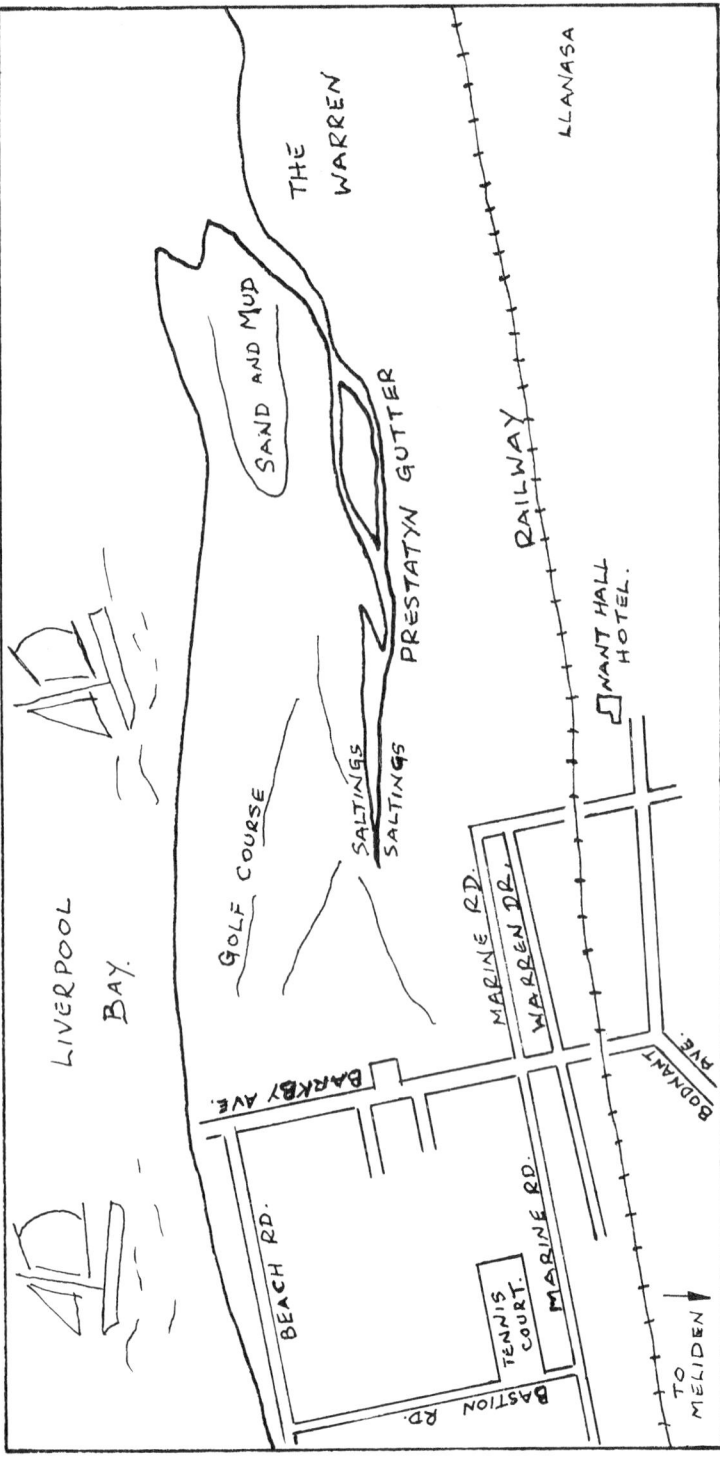

FROM AN OLD MAP OF PRESTATYN SHOWING THE ROADS BUILT BY POCHIN.

BASTION ROAD & BARKBY ROAD WERE BUILT ON THE SITE OF POCHIN'S COBS OR EMBANKMENTS.

(F.HEY)

embankments, or cobs, as they were known locally, at each end of his foreshore property, and into these embankments he suspended doors that could be opened or shut to keep out the sea water or allow the land water to escape. When that operation had been completed he drained the water-logged ground, using windmills specially imported from Holland to work the pumping machinery. The result of all that preparatory work may be seen to-day in the promenade, tennis-courts, bowling greens and car parks that occupy what was once waste ground.

One of Pochin's neighbours in North Wales, and one with whom he occasionally exchanged horticultural specimens, was Sir Edward Watkin, Chairman of the Manchester, Sheffield and Lincolnshire Railway and the Metropolitan Railway Company. It is probable that it was through their friendship that Pochin began to take an interest in railways and eventually acquired a substantial number of shares in both the companies. He became a Director and then a Vice-Chairman of the Metropolitan, and along with Sir Edward is reputed to have saved the Railway from insolvency. In his capacity as a Director of the Metropolitan he displayed the same technological expertise as in all the other companies with which he was associated. During the 1880's he had entered into correspondence with an electrical expert and inventor, Henry Wilde, regarding the feasibility of converting the railway from steam to electric power. Wilde's replies indicated that he did not consider the idea feasible at the time but it was appropriate that when the Metropolitan Railway Company finally became the first British Railway to adopt electrification, it was Pochin's son-in-law, then the first Lord Aberconway who accompanied the Railway's chief engineer on a preliminary survey of the systems in use in Switzerland.

Pochin's last financial involvement, which was connected with railways, was perhaps his least successful one. In the late 1880's, along with Sir Edward Watkin and Capt. Pavey, two of his co-directors on the Metropolitan Railway, he embarked on a scheme to convert Wembley Park, on the outskirts of London, into a great suburban resort complete with winter gardens, facilities for out-door sports and a tower, over 1,000 feet high, that could be used for amusements and scientific purposes such as lectures and exhibitions.

A Company, The Tower Company, with a capital of £300,000 in £1 shares was formed to further the project in 1889 and though there was no official connection between the Company and the Metropolitan Railway, the shareholders of the Railway were informed that a site of 280 acres had been acquired and that their Directors were 'in treaty with the Tower Company to place the great work alongside their line at the particular site.' The Directors of the Metropolitan emphasised that they had put their own money into the scheme and they invited the shareholders to do the same.

By 1895, £70,000 of the Tower Company's authorised capital had been subscribed and £56,000 or 16/- per share called in. In addition, as the Stock Exchange Year Book reported, the foundations of the proposed tower had been constructed along with roads, bridge approaches and an ornamental lake. The grounds also had been carefully laid out, drained and planted and the portions of the estate constituting the proposed tower grounds had been fenced in. Other portions of the estate had been retained for building sites.

The construction of the tower, the design of which had been selected from sixty-eight entries submitted in a public competition, had been placed in the hands of a separate company, The Tower Construction Company, which had a capital of £200,000 and was under the chairmanship of Sir Edward Watkin. By agreement, it had to pay to the Tower Company an annual rental of £2,000.

Seven years after the formation of the mother Company, the first stage of the tower was completed to a height of 200 feet by Heenan & Froude, the builders of the Blackpool Tower, and was thrown open to the public. The result was considered disappointing, only about 18,000 people making the ascent in comparison with the 180,000 who entered the adjoining cycle track and sports ground during the same period of six months. As time went on, many attempts were made to improve the position and the Metropolitan Railway, who of course gained from the site being on their line, came forward with financial support which made little difference to that position. In 1900, the Metropolitan Tower Construction Company, as it had become known, was wound up by voluntary liquidation and its leasehold transferred to the Tower Company in consideration of that Company taking over its debts and liabilities. The Tower Company itself was reconstituted in 1907 and renamed the Wembley Park Estates Company. In that year, too, the foundations of the tower, set in concrete blocks each measuring 26 ft. by 25 ft. were demolished by explosives. Conceived primarily as a financial investment, and written off by some writers of the time as a white elephant, it was the forerunner of the present Wembley Stadium and a tribute to the foresight of its instigators, who, it is fair to say, were not guided solely by their desire to make money. Watkin, Pochin and Pavy were capitalists with a great interest in outdoor sports and scientific knowledge and were anxious, as their records show, that ordinary people should have the opportunity to join in those pursuits. In spite of his reputation for ruthlessness in the board-room, Watkin had supported, along with others, a campaign for a Saturday half-day holiday for the workers in the Manchester district where he was once in business as a merchant.

Photo: Wembley History Society

The Wembley Tower
Designed to reach a height of 1,150 feet, the tower never rose beyond the height of 200 feet at which it was opened to the public in 1896. Pochin was a director of the Wembley Tower Company in 1889 when the scheme was first launched.

CHAPTER IX

Although nearly a hundred miles from his chemical works in Salford, Pochin, when living at Bodnant, made frequent visits there, and to the several new branches his Company had opened. He was constantly on the alert for fresh opportunities, one of which occurred in 1879 when the demand for his Aluminous Cake had decreased in the dyeing industry but had remained at a good level in the paper making trade to which he was also supplying increasing quantities of the china-clay itself. The paper makers used the china-clay as a filling agent, the mechanical incorporation of the clay into the paper stock resulting in the pigment particles being trapped between the fibres to create a closer textured surface of improved brightness, opacity and absorbency.

With such a demand for china-clay, both for his Aluminous Cake and as a filling agent in the paper trade, there were obvious advantages to Pochin in owning his own source of supply, namely, a china-clay mine. But those mines, mainly in Cornwall, had been jealously kept in the hands of their owners, local families and some potters, ever since a Plymouth apothecary, William Cockworthy, had first recognised in the 18th century that the china-stone and china-clay found in Cornwall had properties similar to those of Kao-lin, the material used by the Chinese in the manufacture of their hard porcelain.   However, in 1879 a slump occurred in the Cornish china-clay industry and Pochin was quick to seize the opportunity of acquiring the Gothers Mine in the parish of St. Dennis which had been worked for over seventy years and was then in the hands of William, James, Thomas and Henry Brown of St. Austell.

One modern writer has said that china-clay in the ground is worth practically nothing, its final cost being derived almost exclusively from refining, filtering, drying and transporting.   This was a truth that Pochin realised at an early stage and within a short time of acquiring the Gothers Mine he had constructed a $2\frac{1}{4}$ mile tramway from the mine to the Domellick Siding on the Par-Newquay Railway which carried the clay, when dried, to the china-clay schooners at the ports.   The tramway was also used for the conveyance of coal, which the schooners often brought back as ballast from Runcorn, direct to the mine where it was used as fuel for the washing and drying machinery. An interesting feature of the tramway was that it was laid on sleepers (studded with copper nails) made from the timbers taken from one of the Navy's old wooden ships being broken up at Davenport. The ultimate extent of Pochin's development of Gothers may be judged by the fact that originally the mine produced 50-100 tons of clay annually whereas, thirty years later, it dried and refined over 5,100 tons.

The output from the Gothers Mine contributed substantially to Pochin's need for china-clay but it still fell far short of his total requirements and when, in 1884, the opportunity came to acquire yet another mine he bought the Halviggan and Plain Dealings Mine which was situated on the Halviggan Moors overlooking St. Austell and the English Channel. The clay there produced was eminently suitable for the paper trade and H.D.P. Clay, as it later became known, soon attained a position as one of the best-known clays in the industry.

As at Gothers, he immediately looked around for possible improvement and soon introduced a system whereby the clay-water in the "drags" and settling pits could be conveyed by pipe-line to the dries situated near the Burngullow station on the Great Western Railway, a distance of two miles. This was not only the first line of any considerable length to be laid down for this purpose, but it remained for many years the longest of its kind in Cornwall.

At Halviggan Pochin also constructed a 'dry' capable of turning out 8,000 tons of china-clay per annum and with the two mines in production he was able, at last, to meet the existing demands of both his chemical business and the paper makers. He shipped the clay direct from Cornwall to his works at Bristol, Willington Quay and Manchester, though in the latter case it first went into his warehouse at Runcorn.

In 1883, just before his acquisition of the Halviggan Mine, Pochin had decided that steps should be taken to convert his own chemical company, then managed to a great extent by his brother, William, and other members of the family, into a limited liability Company. Plans were accordingly drawn up in which the Nominal Capital of the new Company was fixed at £110,000, divided into 5,500 shares of £20 each. By a Memorandum of Agreement Pochin transferred the goodwill of his business as a manufacturing chemist, drysalter and china-clay manufacturer, together with his interest in the buildings at Newcastle, Bristol, Newton Heath (Manchester), and Gothers, Cornwall, to the new Company. He also agreed to lease for the Company his works and buildings at Salford for twenty years at a rent of £400 per annum. The new Company, in its turn, agreed to pay him the sum of £89,000 made up of 359 shares of the Company at £20 per share, and 1,800 shares as having had £10 paid on each share. It also agreed to pay him the sum of £63,820, later amended to £64,820 in cash, of which sum £53,820 would be applied in payment of £20 per share on the 2,691 shares subscribed for by Pochin and the other subscribers. By coincidence or design, the difference between the original and amended cash payment to Pochin was exactly the price of the house he purchased for his daughter, Laura McLaren, in London during the same year.

CHAPTER X

In addition to his continuing active interest in the many firms with which he was connected and in the development of the property he had acquired in North Wales, Pochin also enjoyed the greater freedom that his retirement from public life had given him. He was able to follow more closely pursuits which otherwise he would have had to put at one side for lack of time. Gardening was amongst the chief of those but, apart from that, he was a keen student of almost everything connected with science and he once gave a lecture, in North Wales, on "Things Infinitely Great and Things Infinitely Small" which dealt with astronomy on the one hand and microbiology on the other. He was also an enthusiastic archæologist and once, following his return from a visit he had made to Egypt, in 1881, he invited forty of his fellow members of the Cambrian Archæological Society to a luncheon at Bodnant Hall, after which the entire party went to the ancient camp site at Pencaer Helen.

When, in 1886, Professor Boyd Dawkins began his exploration of the Gop Hill tumulus, a huge mound of limestone rubble about six miles from Rhyl, in North Wales, Pochin paid all the expenses of the work on the 820 foot hill that stood on his Prestatyn estate. Another ancient monument, Offa's Dyke, is also reputed to have had its beginning on land owned by Pochin.

Boyd Dawkins took a party, including Pochin, to the Gop Hill site, in 1891, and delivered a lecture on the result of his explorations which despite a great deal of work had produced nothing more than the bones of a few animals. He told the party, all members of the Cambrian Society, that he hoped to make a more extensive examination at some future date and then, rather surprisingly announced that while they had been opening the tumulus Pochin had dug out a fox run on the hillside and in so doing had unearthed the entrance to what was subsequently named the Gop Hill Bone Cave. This had been examined and large quantities of charcoal, the bones and teeth of domestic animals and pieces of rude pottery, adorned with chevron were found. Close against the rock, below an

overhanging ledge of limestone was found a limestone slab which covered the bones of several
human beings, and, to the right of that was a
sepulchral chamber measuring about 4' 6'' square
and 3' 10'' high.   No bronze implements were found
but pottery taken from the chamber was obviously
of a kind manufactured during the bronze age.
Boyd Dawkins said there was no evidence that the
tumulus and the bone cave were connected.   He
further disclosed that in the earth of the cave had
been found the bones of reindeer, rhinoceros and
other animals, all bearing the marks of having been
gnawed by hyenas, whose den it had been.

Pochin, in addition to the intellectual stimulus
provided by his membership of the Cambrian
Archæological Society, also obtained a great deal
of physical enjoyment from the field work of the
Society for, in his younger days he had been a keen
athlete and still derived immense pleasure from
long walks on the Welsh mountains.   When,
however, as he grew older and these became
impossible, he contemplated building a house on
the Llyn Eigiau property, west of Dolgarrog, in
the Snowdon area.   Plans were prepared and a

name, The Eagle's Nest, actually selected for the house, but the project never materialised beyond that point and he had to remain largely content with his estate at Bodnant for his walking. The estate had a steep cliff walk which he had constructed himself and this he never hesitated to climb.

As time went on, Pochin became almost a naturalised Welshman and was appointed a Justice of the Peace, and a Deputy Lieutenant of Denbighshire. Later, he became a Sheriff of that County and attended his first Assizes at Ruthin in 1889. Doubtless as a result of high blood pressure he had suffered all his life from headaches and on the 31st December, 1890, he had a slight stroke from which he quickly recovered. Four years later, however, he became unwell again and after sixteen months of ill health he died, on the 28th October, 1895, at the age of seventy-one, leaving his wife, Agnes, and one surviving daughter, Laura Elizabeth McLaren. His one surviving son, Percival Gerald, who at one time had been studying chemistry at the Atlas Works of John Brown & Co., Sheffield, of which his father was Vice-Chairman, had earlier been entirely disinherited for conduct which private papers confirm, fully warranted that decision. He died in Germany in 1918.

Henry Davis Pochin, who was buried in the mausoleum which he had erected at Bodnant, had had a remarkable life and one which possibly could not have produced the same results in any other period than the one in which he had lived. The opportunities were there and he had seized them with all the energy and enthusiasm at his command. He was an extremely talented and conscientious man, with a great ability for getting things done, who perhaps saw himself, at one time, as a potential statesman and national reformer. He may even have wished, had his political career gone according to plan, to have been remembered as such, but fate decreed otherwise and it is by his gardens at Bodnant that he is remembered to-day. And who can say that that memorial will not prove more lasting and pleasing to future generations?

Henry Davis Pochin was ably supported during the whole of his life by his wife who, like him, had continued with her campaign of reform despite the tragic deaths of their children. She was concerned especially with the emancipation of women and shortly after her marriage, in 1852, had written a pamphlet under the pseudonym of "Justicia", stating her opinions in no uncertain terms. What she claimed was the right of women to (i) vote in the elections of Members of Parliament on the same conditions as the other sex; (ii) vote under the same conditions as men in municipal elections; (iii) have proper accommodation afforded them in both Houses of Parliament to see how public business is carried on; (iv) have the right to the same terms in divorce, the injury being as great to the wife when the husband is unfaithful or adulterous as it is to the husband when the wife is; (v) marriage should not necessarily put a stop to a career previously marked out for a woman; (vi) the education for women should be such as to train them for a career.

In the event it was sixty years before Parliament finally conceded the right of women, though only if over the age of thirty and married or a householder, to the vote, and much longer before society accepted their other claims to equality with men.

When John Bright introduced his Reform Bill, in 1858, she tried, without success, to induce him

97

to include a clause on womens' suffrage but he refused, saying that although he knew no valid argument against womens' suffrage, he thought that in the existing state of public opinion such a clause would do harm to the cause of reform and do no good to the cause of womens' votes.

She persisted with her campaign over the years, lecturing and writing whenever the chance came and in London particularly she appears to have been in great demand. One of her lectures, given before the Clayland Debating Society, in 1870, was published as a pamphlet and from the contents it would seem that her argument about the equality of women had changed to one of superiority. In her lecture she made the conjecture that the size and weight of a woman's brain relative to her stature was greater than that of a man's. A further advantage over a man that a woman had, she said, was a greater activity of brain which enabled her to seize moments which otherwise would be lost to humanity for want of sufficient promptitude. She ended her lecture, however, with the conclusion that women would be pleasanter and more interesting to each other if they were not always striving for the same thing, and if each could live a richer and fuller life. "At present", she concluded, "we are compelled to endure each other's company unfurnished with general subjects of interest and without ideas or knowledge to show, except such as are already possessed about equally by all. Hence we are driven to personal topics which are always apt to degenerate into gossip and slander."

CHAPTER XI

Laura Elizabeth McLaren, Pochin's only surviving daughter, inherited most of her father's property on his death and she and her husband subsequently took up residence at Bodnant Hall. She was a fine artist and a keen horticulturist, and her gardens at Bodnant, and at Antibes, in France, where she had a villa, were rated amongst the most beautiful in Europe. But, as one writer said, "neither the shining terraces at Bodnant, nor the marble splendours of her Provence estate, dulled her generous enthusiasm for great causes and her sympathy for suffering humanity." Like her mother, Agnes Pochin, she was a devoted campaigner for womens' rights and once wrote an eight-page letter to the Manager of the Great

Central Railway Company complaining of the injustice of charging women a penny for what men got free of charge.

When Laura's husband, Charles Benjamin Bright McLaren, was raised to the peerage in 1911 after serving thirty years as a Member of Parliament he took the title of Aberconway because of its, and his, connection with the district in which Bodnant Hall stood. In later life Lord Aberconway, who had been trained as a barrister, turned from law and politics and became well-known as a captain of industry and an authority on more than one branch of engineering. In 1921 he wrote a book "Basic British Industries", which dealt with coal, iron, steel and ships, all subjects on which his father-in-law had been a recognised authority.

Laura and Charles McLaren were happily married for more than fifty years and had four children, the eldest of whom, Henry Duncan McLaren, was allowed to develop his mother's estate at Bodnant during her lifetime. Like his father, he was a barrister, a Member of Parliament and an industrialist. He was also a

member and President of the Royal Horticultural
Society and he continued to take an active interest
in the Bodnant gardens to the end of his life,
planting many of the present trees and shrubs. He
converted Pochin's original lawn into a series of
five terraces, the Rose Terrace, the Croquet
Terrace, the Lily Terrace, the Lower Rose
Terrace and the Canal Terrace. These to-day are
filled with an exotic display of trees, shrubs, bulbs
and flowers which delight the visitors at all seasons.
Begun in 1905, the work took nine years to complete.
During the conversion of the lawn Pochin's original
cedar trees were retained and have now reached a
great size during the hundred years of their growth.
A comparatively recent addition to the garden, the
Pin Mill, was discovered in 1938 by Lord
Aberconway in the village of Woodchester in
Gloucester. The mill was formerly a garden house
in the garden of an Elizabethan manor where the
little factory or mill had been added at a later date.
When discovered much of the wood was still sound
and Lord Aberconway had it dismantled and re-
erected on the Canal Terrace at Bodnant where it
now contains some good Fontainebleau tapestry

Bodnant Gardens, Pin Mill and Canal Terrace

The pin mill was originally constructed as a garden house attached to an Elizabethan residence at Woodchester, Gloucestershire in 1730. It was removed to Bodnant in 1939.

Water Lily Terrace, Bodnant Gardens

dating from 1561. In 1949 he gave part of the gardens, which had formerly been open to the public, to the National Trust, which, by coincidence, had been founded in the same year that Henry Davis Pochin had died.

It was during Henry Duncan McLaren's lifetime that the china-clay producing part of Henry Davis Pochin's old Company, H. D. Pochin & Co., amalgamated with English China Clays, itself already amalgamated with other companies and Loverings, to form English China Clays, Loverings and Pochin's, or E. C. L. P., the largest producers of china-clay in the world. The Chairman of the Company is the present Lord Aberconway, H. D. Pochin's great grandson. The alum producing section of H. D. Pochin & Co., went to Peter Spence Ltd., whose founder was Peter Spence, a rival of Henry Davis Pochin during his search for a cheap source of alumina compounds in the 1850's.

Prestatyn, the tiny North Wales village that Pochin envisaged as a holiday resort and a residential centre has now grown much as he would have wished and his influence on its early development may still be seen in the names of

Bodnant Hall, Main Entrance
The original hall was extensively altered and extended by Pochin in 1875

many of its avenues and roads. Though six-hundred acres of his outlying property was sold by public auction in 1920 and the local Council bought his gas and water undertakings as well as the foreshore he reclaimed in 1885, the family still retains much in the area, including a site upon which they have installed over five-hundred modern caravans and a chapel for the use of the occupants. A further vindication, surely, of a policy of development initiated by him nearly ninety years ago.

Of the two daughters born to Henry Davis Pochin's daughter, Laura, the elder married Sir Edward Johnson-Ferguson of Springkell, Dumfriesshire, and the younger, Sir Henry Norman, a journalist, author and a Member of Parliament whose elder son, Willoughby Norman, is now Chairman of Boots Limited, the well-known manufacturing and retail chemists. By a strange turn of the wheel of fortune Willoughby Norman's company, in 1972, made a bid for Glaxo Ltd., a group of companies that included what was once James Woolley Sons & Co. Ltd., the manufacturing chemists of Manchester. It was with James

Woolley, the founder of that Company, that Willougby Norman's great grandfather, H.D. Pochin, had entered into partnership in 1858.

The story of the Leicestershire man who settled in Manchester to found a business and make a fortune would hardly be complete without a glance at the accomplishment of another member of the family, his great nephew, Cedric W.T. Pochin, The eldest grandson of Henry Davis Pochin's brother William, who managed the chemical works at Salford, Cedric started a business, into which he took his brother Arthur, on almost the exact amount of capital, £600, that his great-uncle had put into the chemical business of Halliday and Pochin in 1849. The business was prepared to tackle anything from the making of plywood lettering for cinema advertisements to office alterations. Its first order was for six tool boxes for Hans Renolds, in 1932, but from that modest beginning in joinery work the business progressed to full-scale building with a turnover, in 1973, of £6,000,000, with work in progress to the value of nearly £16,000,000. Amongst the Company's best-known works are many fine buildings, including that of the Humanities and Physics, as well as the Computer Building, in the new University of Manchester complex. It has also built, almost within sight of Bodnant Gardens, practically the whole of the new extensions to the University of North Wales at Bangor, and a new hospital at Llanfairfechan. Further south, the name of Pochin appears on many fine projects whilst again in Manchester their sign appears on the Central Building of the Manchester Polytechnic.

William Pochin, Henry Davis Pochin's father, was twice married and had nine children by his second wife. The youngest of these, Edward Davis Pochin, who was born in 1845, eventually joined, like his brothers, the chemical firm of H. D. Pochin & Co. , and his grandson, Edward Eric Pochin, C. B. E. , M. D. , became a Director of Clinical Research and Hon. Physician at the University College Hospital, London, and an author of several publications on radiology. A Gifford-Evans prize-winner in 1940, he was also appointed a U. K. Delegate to the U. N. Scientific Committee on the Effects of Atomic Radiation, and was Chairman of an Internation Commission on Radiological Protection.

Thus the seed that William Pochin sowed when first he came North with his eldest son, in the 1840's, continues to bear fruit. In different fields, perhaps, but still under the name of a family seemingly born to survival and success since their arrival at Barkby Hall, Leicestershire, in the early 14th century.

BIBLIOGRAPHY

Aberconway, Lord
  Basic Industries of Great Britain.

Allen, J. Fenwick
  Some Founders of the Chemical Industry.

Ashton, T. S.
  Economic & Social Investigations in Manchester
  (1833-1933).

Barton, R. M.
  A History of the Cornish Clay Industry.

Boase, Frederick
  Modern English Biography.

Cross, C. F. & Bevan, E. J.
  Paper Making.

Hammond, J. L. & B.
  Age of the Chartists.

Henderson, W. O.
  Trade Cycles of the Nineteenth Century.

Kirkby, W.
  A Century of Pharmacy in Manchester.

Lang, David
  Garibaldi.

Martin & Francis
  Industrial and Manufacturing Chemistry.

Mills, W. Haslam
  John Bright and the Society of Friends.

O'Dea, W. T.
  Electric Power.

O'Leary, Cornelious
The Elimination of Corrupt Practices in British Elections.

Patterson, A. Temple
Radical Leicester.

Poole, Braithwaite,
The Commerce of Liverpool.

Read, Donald
Cobden and Bright.
The English Provinces.

Walling, A. J.
Letters of John Bright.
Selection from the Diaries of John Bright.

Woodward, Sir Llewellyn
Age of Reform.

Journal of the Cambrian Archæological Society

Victorian History of the County of Surrey.

Journal of the Manchester Literary & Philosophical Society.

Salford Weekly News.

Leicester Official Guide.

Salford Council Reports.

House of Commons Library (Research Division